MAR 19

THE SCIENCE OF SUPERPOWERS

THE SCIENCE OF
MIND CONTROL AND TELEPATHY

Cathleen Small

Cavendish
Square

New York

Published in 2019 by Cavendish Square Publishing, LLC
243 5th Avenue, Suite 136, New York, NY 10016

Library of Congress Cataloging-in-Publication Data

Names: Small, Cathleen, author.
Title: The science of mind control and telepathy / Cathleen Small.
Description: First edition. | New York : Cavendish Square, [2019] | Series: The science of superpowers | Includes index. | Identifiers: LCCN 2017052045 (print) | LCCN 2017055593 (ebook) | ISBN 9781502638014 (ebook) | ISBN 9781502637994 (library bound) | ISBN 9781502638007 (pbk.)
Subjects: LCSH: Mental suggestion--Juvenile literature. | Telepathy--Juvenile literature. | Brainwashing--Juvenile literature.
Classification: LCC BF1156.S8 (ebook) | LCC BF1156.S8 S63 2019 (print) | DDC 133.8--dc23
LC record available at https://lccn.loc.gov/2017052045

Editorial Director: David McNamara
Editor: Kristen Susienka
Copy Editor: Rebecca Rohan
Associate Art Director: Amy Greenan
Designer: Joe Parenteau
Production Coordinator: Karol Szymczuk
Photo Research: J8 Media

The photographs in this book are used by permission and through the courtesy of: Cover Patrick Mac Sean/PaloAlto/Alamy Stock Photo; Images; p. 3 (and throughout the book) Keith Pomakis/Wikimedia Commons/File:Cumulus Clouds Over Jamaica.jpg/CC BY SA 2.5; p. 4 Caracterdesign/Vetta/Getty Images; p. 7 John Lund/Blend Images/ Getty Images; p. 8 Elijah Nouvelage/AFP/Getty Images; p. 10 CM Dixon/Print Collector/Getty Images; p. 13 Science History Images/Alamy Stock Photo; p. 14 Vladgrin/iStockphoto.com; p. 17 Romanova Natali/Shutterstock.com; p. 18 Yakobchik Viacheslav/Shutterstock.com; p. 21 Keith Bedford/The Boston Globe/Getty Images; p. 23 Epromocja/E+/Getty Images; p. 24 Lisa Wiltse/Corbis/Getty Images; p. 27 Gwen Shockey/Science Source; p. 29 DigitalVision/Getty Images; p. 31 Thailand Wildlife/Alamy Stock Photo; p. 33 Pavlina Popovska/Shutterstock.com; p. 34 David Ramos/Getty Images; p. 36 George Dolgikh/Shutterstock.com; p. 39 Benny Marty/Shutterstock.com; p. 41 PA Images/Alamy Stock Photo; p. 43 Coneyl Jay/Science Photo Library/Getty Images.

Printed in the United States of America

CONTENTS

CHAPTER 1

THE HISTORY OF MIND CONTROL AND TELEPATHY

T here are many examples of superheroes who can control someone's actions or thoughts. Sometimes, a superhero sends a message to a person using their minds. Other times, they make someone do something for them

Opposite: This man is trying to use a form of mind control called hypnosis.

by taking over the person's mind for a little while. These superheroes are using the powers of mind control and telepathy.

WHAT ARE MIND CONTROL AND TELEPATHY?

In mind control, one person tries to influence or control another person's thoughts. Telepathy means someone is trying to send a message or move information from one person's brain to another person's brain. Sometimes, telepathy is easier to do than mind control. For example, people can speak without words. Two people who see each other across a room may not actually speak. They may give **nonverbal** cues, such as a smile or a wave. Still, they are saying "hello" to each other.

When telepathy influences another person's thoughts or beliefs, it is called mind control. Advertising companies use a form of mind control. Companies advertise products using bright colors, catchy words, famous people, and other ways to help convince people to buy from them. They are not only sending information from the company's advertisers into the brains of buyers. They are using sales strategies to try to influence buyers.

Telepathy is transferring thoughts from one person's brain into another's.
This photograph imagines what that might look like.

Mind control and telepathy are similar topics, but they are not exactly the same thing. Mind control involves influence and can include outside props or strategies to achieve its goal. Telepathy is simply transferring information from one person's brain to another person's brain.

HISTORY OF TELEPATHY

The history of telepathy goes back to the ancient Egyptians and Greeks. Egyptians believed in

In a simple form of mind control, companies use eye-catching advertisements to try to persuade people to buy their products.

something called **dream incubation**. That meant that a spirit would send messages from one person to another in dreams. The Greeks also believed dreams were a way to send messages.

Modern interest in telepathy began in 1819, when a man named H.M. Weserman published the results of a study he did on influencing thinking and dreams. Weserman claimed success in five experiments about controlling what people saw in dreams. However, he admitted that in at least one case, the participant dreamed about a related topic, rather than what Weserman had intended.

In 1882, Frederic W.H. Myers helped start the Society of Psychical Research (SPR). This organization was dedicated to studying psychic and paranormal events, abilities, and activities. The theories put forth by SPR were met with **skepticism** from the scientific community. Some thought the work the SPR did lacked scientific backing.

DID YOU KNOW?

Twins are often thought to have a telepathic link. There are many stories of one twin knowing what's going on with the other, even when they're far apart. While there is no scientific evidence supporting twin telepathy, many twins report having these experiences.

The field of telepathy grew again in 1930 when American author Upton Sinclair published the book *Mental Radio*. He wrote about his and his wife Mary's attempts to test telepathy. It was rumored that Mary had telepathic abilities. To test her, Sinclair created telepathy tests. One test involved him and others creating 290 sketches. Mary supposedly did not see them. However, when asked to draw whatever came to mind, she could duplicate them in sixty-five instances, even when she was miles away from the person creating the sketch. Sinclair was a respected author, so many took his book seriously. But others pointed out that his experiments hadn't been done in a laboratory with appropriate **controls**, so the results weren't necessarily accurate.

HISTORY OF MIND CONTROL

Mind control has a much longer history than telepathy. The oldest form of mind control is trephination. It was a physical example of mind control. Trephination meant a hole was drilled into a person's skull. Skulls dating back to 6500 BCE show evidence of trephination. People thought the hole would release evil spirits from the brain. In reality, many people who had this surgery done were likely suffering from a mental illness.

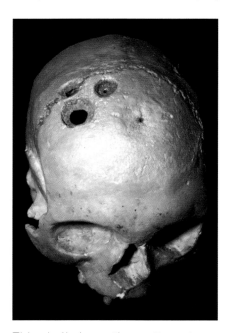
This skull shows three attempts at trephination.

In the 1400s, many people were believed to be witches. In reality, these "witches" probably suffered from an undiagnosed mental illness. A book called *The Malleus Maleficarum* was published in 1487. It gave tips on how to identify witches and how to question them. The questions were meant to get them to admit they were witches. In other words, people following *The Malleus Maleficarum* influenced confessions by trying to get the supposed witches to say what they wanted to hear. Influencing confessions can be a form of mind control because sometimes the person confessing actually starts to wonder if what they're saying is true. It can be surprisingly easy to make someone believe a specific story or event if you ask the right questions!

Treatments for mental illness in the nineteenth century also involved mind control. Some doctors tried to change the way people thought by shocking them. This was called shock therapy. Some doctors believed that mental illness was caused by problems in the brain. They had seen that sometimes head injuries, fever, or seizures could change how a person thought. They believed that shocking someone might have the same effect. The expected outcome was that it would

Early Shock Treatments

Shock therapy is still done today, though not very often. It's used only after most other treatments for mental illness have failed.

Years ago, shock therapy was used more often. One early form of shock therapy was water-shock treatment. The person being treated was blindfolded and left standing on a platform. Without warning, the platform would collapse. The individual would fall into a pool of ice water.

Noise-shock treatment was another kind of treatment. A person was blindfolded and stood outside. Then, without warning, someone would fire a cannon behind them. This would send a shock to the person and affect their hearing.

Perhaps most surprisingly, shock treatments existed before modern electricity was developed. There are certain fish whose bodies carry an electrical charge. Ancient Greeks, Romans, and Egyptians used the electricity from these fish as one of the earliest shock-therapy treatments.

improve the patient's mental health. In reality, these "treatments" only upset and hurt people.

The nineteenth century also brought interest in hypnotism. In a hypnotized state of mind, people no longer entirely control their thoughts. They are easily persuaded by other people. Hypnosis is a therapy technique that people use to manage pain and sometimes stop bad habits, such as smoking. However, in the 1800s and 1900s, hypnosis was sometimes used for entertainment purposes. An example of this was when a hypnotist would convince a person from an audience to cluck like a chicken or bark like a dog. It's not known whether those people were *really* hypnotized, but it is a common therapy method and an example of mind control.

This 1846 engraving shows a hypnotist attempting to hypnotize a woman.

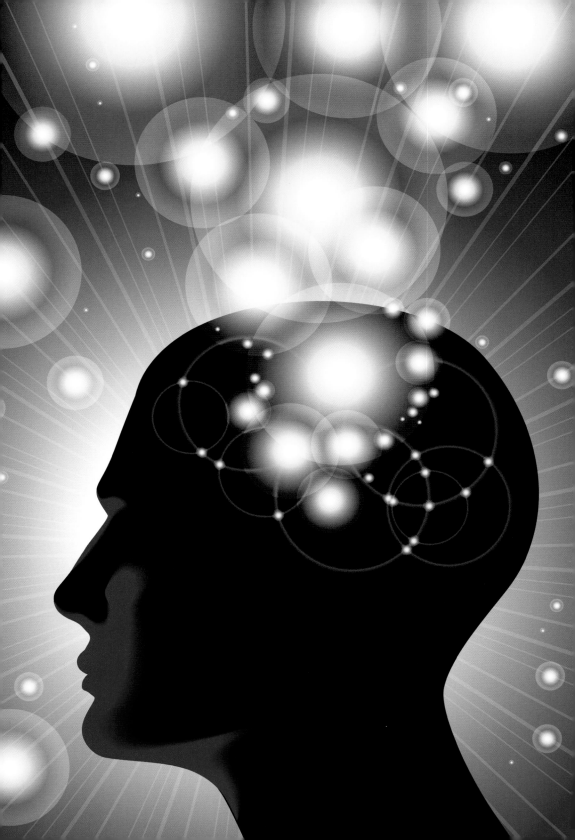

CHAPTER 2

HOW ARE MIND CONTROL AND TELEPATHY POSSIBLE?

T he ideas of mind control and telepathy are tempting! Imagine being able to control someone else's mind! Imagine being able to send thoughts to another

Opposite: Mind control and telepathy seem like superpowers, but are they really possible?

person without even speaking a word. If mind control were possible, lawyers could control jury outcomes, politicians could make people vote for them, and kids could make their parents do whatever they wanted!

But is this possible, or is it just the stuff of myth and legend? Could mind control and telepathy really ever happen? Science suggests they could.

NEUROSCIENCE AND TELEPATHY

Starting around 2013, several groups of researchers began experimenting with telepathy. These researchers worked in an area of science called neuroscience. Neuroscientists study the brain and how it works. In their experiments, the researchers had some positive results with a process known as synaptic transmission.

The brain is part of the nervous system. This system houses all the nerve cells in the body. Synapses are where nerve cells in the body meet. The synapses carry chemical and electrical signals throughout the brain and body. Normally, this is done without the person even thinking about it. For example, when a person moves their arm, the brain sends a message to the arm to move. That

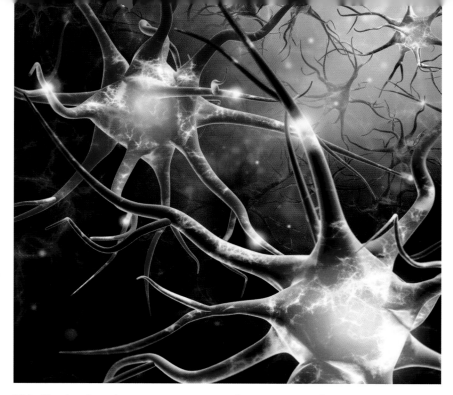

This illustration shows synapses carrying messages between neurons.

message is carried over the brain's synapses. The person doesn't think about moving their arm. It just happens because the brain sees that the arm needs to move and sends the message.

When neuroscientists wanted to create telepathy between two human beings, they focused on synapses and how they send messages. They attached special **electrodes** to a helmet. The helmet was worn by a person in the experiment. The electrodes could read the brain activity of the person wearing the helmet. In one test, the

How Are Mind Control and Telepathy Possible? **17**

person was giving a greeting. In another test, the person was making a hand movement. The electrodes read the activity going on in the brain of the person performing the activity. That activity was then translated into **binary code** and sent to another person far away. In one case, the other person was 5,000 miles (8,046 kilometers) away!

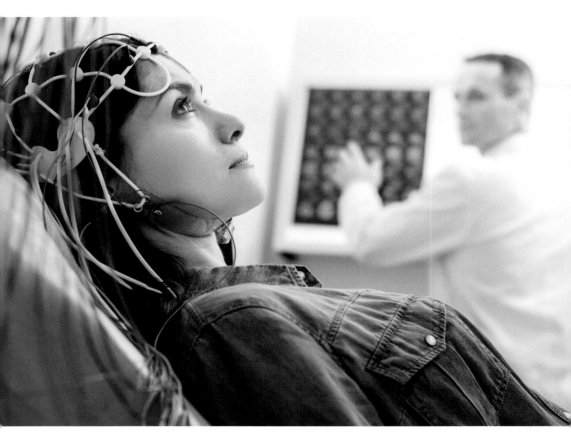

Electrodes like these on the woman's head can read a person's brain activity.

On the receiving end, the coded messages were decoded. Then, the decoded messages were fed to the receiving person's brain using a process known as transcranial magnetic stimulation (TMS).

The technology didn't work perfectly, but it worked well enough for researchers to believe they were closer to creating telepathy. According to researchers, this type of development could be useful for soldiers on the battlefield who need to receive instructions from a commanding officer or from another soldier. Businesspeople could also communicate without words during a sales pitch. It could also be a communication method for people who are unable to speak.

NEUROSCIENCE AND MIND CONTROL

To some scientists, the process by which neuroscientists are imitating telepathy is proof

The Technology Behind Telepathy

Two technologies used to receive and send messages are electroencephalograms (EEGs) and transcranial magnetic stimulations (TMSs). EEG technology has been around since the late 1800s. Patients wear electrodes on their scalp. These electrodes read electrical activity in the brain. EEGs help doctors diagnose seizures, sleep disorders, and brain death.

In TMS, doctors and scientists send electrical currents to the brain using a small coil. This might sound like a frightening treatment, but it actually isn't. It is painless and sometimes used to treat depression. It can also be used to see whether a that mind control is possible. The studies done by neuroscientists on brain-to-brain communication only transmitted simple information, such as a greeting or the suggestion to move a hand. However, they say the same technology could be used to control the thoughts or actions of another person.

There are two parts to mind control, though. There is sending messages from one person to

person's brain has been damaged by strokes or similar disorders. TMS is a newer technology than EEG. It has only been approved for use in the past ten years.

TMS devices send electrical currents to the brain.

However, there are concerns about these technologies. If used improperly, they could intrude on a person's privacy. Also, some scientists argue that they are not true telepathy. True telepathy involves brain-to-brain communication with no outside influence. While TMS and EEG technologies are noninvasive, they are still outside influences on the process. To some scientists, they are *imitating* telepathy, but not really performing it.

another and then there is information-based mind control, which is much harder to manage. Information-based mind control is when information outside of the person's brain affects a person's thinking or emotions. For example, when people watch sad movies or read sad books, they often feel sad afterward. When they hear upbeat, happy music, it can often lift their mood.

This type of mind control is used all the time. Advertisers and salespeople use it a lot. They play on people's emotions to try to get a desired outcome. But it's also used by ordinary people every day. For example, children who don't want to go to bed at night are famous for playing on their parents' emotions by crying or saying things like, "I'm scared!" or "I miss you!" They hope that their parent will feel guilty and allow them to stay awake a bit longer.

This sort of mind control happens so much that we don't even think about it! That's why it's so effective. It's also why it's so uncontrollable. Scientists may be able to learn how to send messages from one person's brain to another, but they cannot stop people from being influenced by outside sources. For that reason, true mind control will be very difficult to ever achieve.

Pictures like this one of a sad puppy are designed to make people feel certain emotions.

So will mind control and telepathy ever really be possible? It seems likely that they will to some extent. However, full mind control is unlikely to happen since we see outside influences all day, every day.

CHAPTER 3

REAL-LIFE EXAMPLES OF MIND CONTROL AND TELEPATHY

Mind control and telepathy aren't all just myth and science fiction. Science has proven that to some extent, both may be possible in the future. But it's equally interesting to learn about real-life examples of telepathy and mind control!

Opposite: Some people believe that twins have a special telepathic link.

TWIN TELEPATHY

There have been many stories of twins who are particularly connected to each other. There's even a saying—"it's a twin thing"—that is often used to describe this close connection twins can have.

Not all twins have it. Some report they have no more connection to their twin than to any other person they know well. In a 2004 poll of nine thousand twins, 15 percent reported having twin telepathy, and another 39 percent said they thought they might have it. Of the twins who believe in a telepathic link, they say that if one twin is hurt or sad, the other twin can feel it, even if he or she is far away.

In one famous 2009 case, a British teenager named Gemma Houghton suddenly had a strong feeling that her twin sister, Leanne, needed help. At the time, Leanne was taking a bath upstairs in the closed bathroom. Gemma went in to check on her sister and discovered that Leanne had had a seizure and was unconscious under the bathwater.

In another case, a mother of twin boys took the twins to the doctor when one kept complaining of pain in his kidney area. The doctor couldn't find anything wrong with the boy's kidney, but then he

The Science of Twins

All babies form from an egg. With twins, one of two things can happen. Either two different eggs grow at the same time into two completely separate babies or one single egg can split into two and then develop into two different babies.

When two eggs are present right from the beginning, the twins are fraternal. When one egg splits into two, the twins are identical. When identical twins develop, the egg can split into two anywhere from one to twelve days into the process of human development. Researchers at the University of Indiana have done studies on thousands of twins and have determined that the later the egg splits into two, the more closely connected the twins seem to be after birth. So, it's thought that the twins who believe they experience a telepathic connection are likely the twins whose egg split later in the development process.

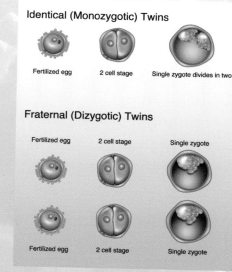

Identical (Monozygotic) Twins

Fertilized egg   2 cell stage   Single zygote divides in two

Fraternal (Dizygotic) Twins

Fertilized egg   2 cell stage   Single zygote

Fertilized egg   2 cell stage   Single zygote

In the top image, one egg divides and becomes identical twins. In the bottom one, fraternal twins develop from two separate eggs.

checked the boy's twin brother. He found that the boy had a serious kidney problem, even though he hadn't been feeling any pain.

There are far more twin telepathy stories than just these. In fact, there are so many that although science has not proven such a strong link between twins, many believe that one exists.

MIND CONTROL IN THE REAL WORLD

In the real world, information-based mind control takes place all the time. Any time one person tries to influence another person's feelings or decisions, it's a form of mind control. Often there's nothing negative about this type of mind control. For example, a teacher might try to convince his or her students that math is fun by making the subject exciting.

However, sometimes information-based mind control can be a problem. For example, **cults** sometimes use mind control to get new members to join. They compliment potential new members and give them a lot of attention to make them feel welcome. Then, when the new members are firmly a part of the cult, they are encouraged to stop talking to friends and family members who aren't part of the cult.

One positive use of mind control is when teachers use enthusiasm to get students excited about learning.

A condition called Stockholm syndrome is a form of mind control too. This happens when kidnappers form a bond with the person they've kidnapped. They are eventually able to get their victim to feel as if their kidnapper is somehow doing them a favor or cares about them. That, too, is a type of mind control. It's a rare situation, but it does occur.

Aside from information-based mind control, there are other ways mind control can happen. One example is a lobotomy. In a lobotomy, a surgeon cuts connections in part of the brain. Lobotomies used to be done on patients suffering from various mental illnesses. It changed how the patient thought from that point forward. However, this operation is rarely done any more.

MIND CONTROL AND ANIMALS

In the animal kingdom, mind control exists too. There is a type of fungus called *Ophiocordyceps* that takes over the minds and bodies of certain kinds of ants. It does this to complete its life cycle.

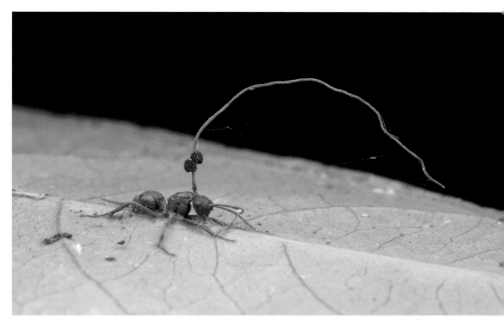

This zombie ant has a stalk growing out of its head that will spread more of the fungus that infected it.

It basically makes the ants into zombie ants. When the ants come across the fungus while looking for food, the fungal cells make their home in the ant's head and then spread throughout the ant's body. The fungal cells then force the ant to climb up on a leaf or twig and clamp down. When that is done, the fungus slowly kills the ant and grows a stalk out of the back of its head. The stalk is used to spread more fungal spores onto the ground below. Then more ants will eat the fungus and become infected.

The parasite *Toxoplasma gondii* can live in any warm-blooded animal, but it only reproduces in the bodies of cats. Humans can be exposed to it if they are around cats that have the parasite. However, in healthy humans the infection from the parasite normally causes a mild flu-like illness. In rodents, though, it causes changes in behavior and personality that are similar to mind control.

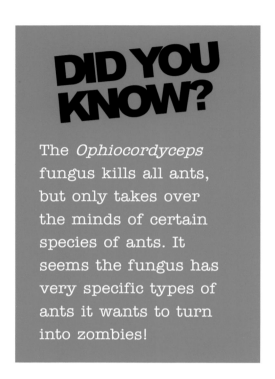

DID YOU KNOW?

The *Ophiocordyceps* fungus kills all ants, but only takes over the minds of certain species of ants. It seems the fungus has very specific types of ants it wants to turn into zombies!

Rodents normally avoid areas where cats live, since cats like to hunt them. But rodents affected by the *Toxoplasma gondii* parasite do not avoid areas where cats live. The reason for this seems to be brain changes that happen because of the infection. For this reason, rodents affected by the parasite are more likely to be killed by cats, since they have lost their natural instinct to avoid cats.

Toxoplasma gondii reproduces in the bodies of cats and can cause humans exposed to it to become mildly ill.

While full-on mind control isn't known to have occurred yet, there's no doubt that in subtle ways, humans and animals sometimes find their minds to be manipulated.

CHAPTER 4

MODERN AND FUTURE EXPLORATIONS OF MIND CONTROL AND TELEPATHY

Mark Zuckerberg, the founder of Facebook, commented in 2015 that he believes the future of communication is in telepathy. He thinks technology will be the key to sending thoughts directly to other people. While it might sound like a distant dream, he may not be wrong.

Opposite: Facebook's founder, Mark Zuckerberg, is interested in exploring telepathy as it relates to technology.

DEVELOPMENTS IN TELEPATHY AND MIND CONTROL TECHNOLOGY

At the University of California at Berkeley in 2011, scientists performed a study where they reconstructed movie clips watched by participants in the study. The reconstructions were based only on the measurements researchers took of participants' brainwaves. The reconstructed

Rats are often used in scientific research, such as studies being done on telepathy.

clips weren't perfect, but they were close enough to accurately represent what general clips the participants had watched.

In 2013, researchers at Duke University in North Carolina inserted electrodes into lab rats. These electrodes were designed to send **neural** signals. The results were promising. The researchers had taught one rat how to press one of two levers. Then they put the second rat in front of the same set of two levers. The second rat seemed to know which lever to push, even though the second rat had not been trained. This evidence suggests that the second rat may have successfully received the neural signals from the first rat.

The likelihood of humans wanting electrodes planted into their brains is slim, so most research is focusing on noninvasive options. For example, the US Army is developing a telepathy helmet that would allow brain-to-brain communication. Some researchers are also considering using handheld MRI machines that would allow people to capture their own brain activity, which could then be transmitted to others.

What Is Building 8?

The buildings that house Facebook's headquarters are on a large campus in California. The complex is visible from the main road, and there isn't much mystery about it. However, one mysterious part of it is a research lab called Building 8. Not much is known about what projects are being developed at the company. But Facebook has several scientists and technology experts working for them.

One new technology could involve reading people's minds. A neuroscientist works for the company. He is known for inventing a mind-operated prosthetic arm. Building 8 might be working on more mind-controlled technology, including computers. Job postings for positions in Building 8 seem to be looking for employees whose skills relate to telepathy and technology.

Only time will tell what's really going on there. But if Facebook is successful in implementing brain-to-brain communication, maybe they won't even have to tell the public what's going on—the public will just know!

The Facebook campus in California, shown here, is home to the mysterious Building 8.

MIND CONTROL FOR MEDICAL TREATMENT

Although some people wonder if we should be trying to control other people's thoughts, medical researchers have been inventing devices that have helped people control other things with their minds. One example is BrainPort. This technology helps blind people "see" again. Users wear a tiny video camera, carry around a laptop computer, and put sensors on their tongue. The camera records the images in front of the person. The laptop interprets the images and sends a signal to the sensors to tingle the tongue. The brain of the blind person then reads these tingles to "see" what's in front of them. The device doesn't restore their vision, but still it allows them to "see."

Another new technology, called

DID YOU KNOW?

One group of people who might be interested in brain implants is people who have lost limbs. Researchers think implants may allow people to use their brain to control a robotic limb, such as an arm or a leg.

BrainGate, is a tiny device inserted into the brain. It is being tested by a team of researchers at Massachusetts General Hospital. It is helping people who have lost the use of their arms and

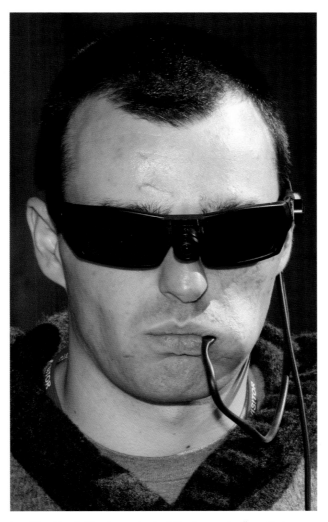

Technologies like BrainPort can help blind people "see" via sensors placed on their tongue.

legs. One paralyzed woman who uses a BrainGate implant has spent more than one thousand days accurately moving a cursor on her computer screen and pointing-and-clicking to allow the computer to perform various tasks. Given that she has no use of her arms, this activity would not be possible without the implant. BrainGate2 is also being tested for helping people move robotic limbs and control wheelchairs.

THE FUTURE

While telepathy and mind control may sound like the stuff of superheroes and science-fiction characters, in reality, it isn't so farfetched. How and where it will be used in the future remains to be seen, but the technology is developing rapidly. It may not be long before telepathy and mind control become even more apparent in everyday life.

This is one artist's interpretation of telepathy. Only time will tell what the future holds in telepathy and mind control development!

Modern and Future Explorations of Mind Control and Telepathy **43**

GLOSSARY

BINARY CODE A coding system that uses 0s and 1s to represent letters, digits, or characters.

CONTROL An item or group to which experiment results are compared.

CULT A group of people who share common beliefs or practices that are usually considered odd by the rest of society.

ELECTRODE A conductor that allows electricity to enter or leave an object or region.

NEURAL Relating to the nervous system.

NONVERBAL Using actions like eye or hand movement instead of words to speak.

SKEPTICISM Doubt of the truth of an issue.

FIND OUT MORE

BOOKS

Chudler, Eric H. *Brain Lab for Kids: 52 Mind-Blowing Experiments, Models, and Activities to Explore Neuroscience.* Beverly, MA: Quarry Books, 2018.

Olson, Elsie. *Are You Psychic?: Facts, Trivia, and Quizzes.* Minneapolis, MN: Lerner Publishing Group, 2018.

Wynne, Patricia J., and Donald M. Silver. *My First Book About the Brain.* Mineola, NY: Dover Publications, 2013.

WEBSITES

BrainFacts
http://www.brainfacts.org

This website was designed to be a source of information about the brain and nervous system. While the site is designed for adults, it has many articles and links of interest to children and teens.

Neuroscience for Kids
http://faculty.washington.edu/chudler/neurok.html

This website created by the University of Washington has links to a lot of interesting information about the brain and nervous system, as well as developments in neuroscience.

INDEX

ABOUT THE AUTHOR

Cathleen Small is an editor of hundreds of books and the author of dozens of nonfiction books for students. She has written on a variety of topics and is particularly interested in matters of the brain. Small has two neurodiverse sons and has spent much time studying the learning patterns of neurodiverse children. When she's not writing, editing, or researching, Small likes to travel with her family. They live in the San Francisco Bay Area in California.